Algarve
Travel Guide

Quick Trips Series

No part of this publication may be reproduced, stored in a retrieval system, or transmitted, in any form or by any means without the prior written permission of the publisher, nor be otherwise circulated in any form of binding or cover other than that in which it is published and without similar condition being imposed on the subsequent purchaser. If there are any errors or omissions in copyright acknowledgements the publisher will be pleased to insert the appropriate acknowledgement in any subsequent printing of this publication. Although we have taken all reasonable care in researching this book we make no warranty about the accuracy or completeness of its content and disclaim all liability arising from its use.

Copyright © 2016, Astute Press
All Rights Reserved.

Table of Contents

THE ALGARVE — 6
- Customs & Culture 8
- Geography 10
- Weather & Best Time to Visit 11

SIGHTS & ACTIVITIES: WHAT TO SEE & DO — 14
- Lagos 14
  - Antigo Mercado de Escravos (Slave Market) 17
  - Church of St. Sebastian (Igreja de Sao Sebastiao) 18
  - Church of St. Anthony (Igreja de Santo Antonio) 19
  - Zoo Lagos 19
- Tavira 20
  - Tavira Castle 22
- Portimão 23
- Faro 24
  - Faro Archaeological Museum 26
  - Igreja do Carmo Church / Capela dos Ossos (Chapel of Bones) 26
  - Estoi Palace 27
  - Milreu 27
- Ria Formosa 28
- Vilamoura 30
- Albufeira 31
- Monchique 32
- Silves 33

Silves Castle 35
Cork Museum 36
Archaeological Museum 37
🌐 LOULE 37
Convento do Espírito Santo 39
🌐 NEOLITHIC SITES 40

BUDGET TIPS   42

🌐 ACCOMMODATION 42
Tivoli Lagos Hotel 43
Casa das Oliveiras 44
Hotel Porta Nova 45
Hotel Sol Algarve 45
Hotel Ibis Faro 46
🌐 PLACES TO EAT 47
Oasis 47
Marco's Bistro 48
Fat Cats Diner 49
Restaurante a Taska 49
Restaurante da Bairrada 50
🌐 SHOPPING 51
Shopping in Albufeira 51
Shopping in Lagos 52
Shopping in Faro 53
Casa das Portas in Tavira 54
Gypsy Markets 54

KNOW BEFORE YOU GO   56

🌐 ENTRY REQUIREMENTS 56
🌐 HEALTH INSURANCE 56
🌐 TRAVELLING WITH PETS 57
🌐 AIRPORTS 58
🌐 AIRLINES 59

- Currency 60
- Banking & ATMs 60
- Credit Cards 60
- Tourist Taxes 61
- Reclaiming VAT 61
- Tipping Policy 62
- Mobile Phones 62
- Dialling Code 63
- Emergency Numbers 63
- Public Holidays 64
- Time Zone 64
- Daylight Savings Time 65
- School Holidays 65
- Trading Hours 65
- Driving Laws 66
- Drinking Laws 67
- Smoking Laws 67
- Electricity 68
- Tourist Information (TI) 68
- Food & Drink 69
- Websites 70

ALGARVE TRAVEL GUIDE

The Algarve

The Algarve, located on the south coast of Portugal, is the country's most popular vacation destination. With two hundred kilometres of sandy beaches and seaside, the Algarve is surprisingly cheap, very safe and rich in culture and diversity.

The sunbathed Portuguese coast is conveniently located just 2-4 hours flight from the colder climates of Northern Europe. The waters of the Algarve are ideal for swimming, and many of the beaches feature interesting coves, cliffs and other rock formations to provide interesting and unique sights both above and below the water line.

ALGARVE TRAVEL GUIDE

There are a number of interesting limestone caves and lagoons that are well worth exploring. Best known of these is the extended lagoon known as Ria Formosa.

Water sports are not the only activities to pursue, when on vacation here. The region has great facilities for a number of other sporting activities, such as horseriding, tennis, cycling and golf.

The Algarve has a number of superb golf courses, reckoned to be among the finest on the European continent. The golf course at Vilamoura has hosted the Portuguese Masters Golf Tournament for several years, attracting the world's top ranking players each year. This location was designed by the American legend, Arnold Palmer, who was nicknamed 'The King' in his heyday and

ALGARVE TRAVEL GUIDE

is still considered to be one of the Big Three of golf. Elsewhere, you will find courses designed by greats such as Nick Faldo.

The region of the Algarve has seen settlement since Neolithic times. As the Phoenicians ventured throughout the Mediterranean, they established ports around 1000 BC. In its long and extensive history, the Algarve region has seen occupation by Phoenicians, Romans, Visigoths and Moors. Even after the re-conquest by Christian forces, raids from Africa remained a problem till the 1500s.

It was largely from a need to protect the integrity of its coastal settlements that the Portuguese began to embark on a campaign of conquest in the Northwestern parts of

ALGARVE TRAVEL GUIDE

Africa. This brought the country both prestige and considerable wealth through trade, but in 1755 a large earthquake wreaked devastation throughout Portugal. The Algarve did not escape its impact and for this reason, very few complete buildings dating before the disaster survived.

🌍 Customs & Culture

Today's Algarve is friendly and a mainstream tourist destination and the lifestyle here is relaxed and easy-going. Fishing has played a large role in the local economy and continues to do so. For this reason, the traditional cuisine shows a strong preference towards seafood. A fisherman's boat is his pride and joy, which often shows in the decoration lavished upon it. Religion

ALGARVE TRAVEL GUIDE

plays an important role and well over 90 percent of the inhabitants are Catholic.

Many local traditions have remained virtually unchanged for centuries, yet there is a sizable population of English-speaking residents, both temporary and semi-permanent. The lifestyle is relaxed and tranquil.

While many towns have developed to fully-fledged resort locations, some of the village charm remains intact in the cobbled streets, the historic district and in the regular markets, sometimes referred to as gypsy markets.

In the summer months, the region hosts various cultural and religious festivals, including the famous one in Loule, an International Music Festival and a National Folklore

ALGARVE TRAVEL GUIDE

Festival that includes events in different locations across the Algarve. Alcoutim showcases local crafts in a Handicraft Festival in July, while Cacela Velha showcases the Muslim heritage in an event called Moorish Nights. Basketmaking and pottery are local crafts.

Geography

The Algarve is in the southwestern part of the Iberian Peninsula. It is a narrow strip of land, which occupies the entire southern coast of Portugal, from the border with Spain in the east and past the southernmost tip of Europe at Cape St Vincent. From there, it sweeps northwards on the western side for some 52 km. At its widest segments, the Algarve reaches about 36 km inland. It is bounded by the Alentejo region to the north.

ALGARVE TRAVEL GUIDE

Much of the coast of the Algarve is characterized by the combination of attractive beaches flanked by dramatic cliff faces. Towards the northern part, the land steadily rises in ranges of gently rounded hills and mountains.

The region is serviced by Faro airport, which connects to various major destinations around the world. A railway system runs roughly parallel to the coast, reaching from Vila Real do Santo António in the east to Lagos in the Western Algarve. This rail network also connects the region to the rest of Portugal via Lisbon.

By road, the Algarve was bisected by the EN 125, a road that ran from East to West along the entire coast. In recent years, this has been replaced by a newer motorway, the A22. A network of bus services connect different parts of the Algarve.

🌐 Weather & Best Time to Visit

The Algarve enjoys a pleasant, sunny climate that is ideal for beach and outdoor activities. The warmest months are July and August, when maximum temperatures hover around 28 to 29 degrees Celsius and nights can be expected to be fairly warm, with minimums of around 23 to 24 being typical.

In the winter months of December and January, day temperatures will average around 16 to 17 degrees Celsius, with nightly temperatures dropping to between 8 and 9 degrees Celsius.

ALGARVE TRAVEL GUIDE

These are averages for the whole region and the temperatures in individual towns and cities may vary slightly, although not by a wide margin. Faro, for example, sees average summer highs of up to 29 degrees and on individual days, the mercury may rise even higher to reach above 30 degrees Celsius. The sea temperature is typically around 20 degrees Celsius in summer and it may drop to around 16 degrees Celsius in winter.

Rainfall is scarce and can mainly be expected in the winter months between November and March. Even at the height of winter, you will still see sunny days for much of the time.

The best off-season periods to visit will be during the latter part of spring or the earliest period of autumn. In

ALGARVE TRAVEL GUIDE

May, the temperatures average between 22 degrees Celsius in the daytime, dropping to around 13 degrees Celsius at night. Even the month of October still sees averages between 23 and 15 degrees Celsius.

ALGARVE TRAVEL GUIDE

Sights & Activities: What to See & Do

 Lagos

The town of Lagos had been settled for over 2000 years, but its golden era had been the years between 1420 and 1460, when it played a huge part in altering the fortunes of the Algarve and Portugal as a whole. Lagos had been inhabited by Carthaginians, Romans, Visigoths,

ALGARVE TRAVEL GUIDE

Byzantines and Moors, but it is best remembered as the location from which the illustrious Age of Discovery was launched.

Prince Henry the Navigator, the third son of King John of Portugal, was born in 1394. From a relatively young age, he was motivated by the possibility of rich trade on the African continent, especially after the Portuguese capture of Ceuta, a port in Morocco that had served as a base for Barbary raids into Portugal.

When Henry was appointed as the Governor of Algarve, he based himself on the Sagres Peninsula and a number of innovations in sea travel resulted, such as the development of a lighter vessel called a caravel and new insights on cartography.

ALGARVE TRAVEL GUIDE

Gil Eanes, an early Portuguese explorer who was first to round the West African peninsula of Cape Bojador in 1435, was a native of Lagos. This early achievement in the service of Prince Henry the Navigator played an important role in later voyages of the Age of Discovery.

Both Gil Eanes and Prince Henry the Navigator are honored with statues, Henry's being in the vicinity of Praça da República. Other statues in Lagos are that of São Gonçalo on Avenida dos Descobrimentos, honoring the region's only homegrown saint and Dom Sebastiao on the Main Square.

Some notable buildings of Lagos are the Governor's Castle or Castelo dos Governadores, with some walls

ALGARVE TRAVEL GUIDE

dating back to Moorish times and Forte da Ponta da Bandeira.

Today, Lagos is a popular stop for tourists. It has several beautiful and accessible beaches. Meia Praia with its beach bars and boardwalk is popular with tourists. The crowded Praia da Batata is conveniently located right by the town center and offers conveniences such as sun beds, water sporting opportunities and the views of Forte Ponta da Bandeira. Praia da Dona Ana can be reached by a series of wooden steps and is surrounded by majestic cliff and rock formations. Another beach worth a visit, not only for its unusual rock structures, but also the surrounding flora and impressive caves nearby, is Ponta da Piedade.

ALGARVE TRAVEL GUIDE

The marina at Lagos offers the opportunity for boat tours and dolphin watching. A boat trip also enables a unique view of Ponta da Piedada's unusual features and its lighthouse. Lovers of water sport can enjoy activities such as diving, kayaking or sailing, while Lagos also has excellent facilities for tennis, Go-karting, land sailing, golf and horse-riding. There is a Slide and Splash water park a mere 20 minutes away from Lagos.

Antigo Mercado de Escravos (Slave Market)

Praca do Infante Dom Henriques, Lagos, Portugal

Now a small art gallery, this was once the site where fierce trade in human stock took place during Portugal's Age of Discovery.

ALGARVE TRAVEL GUIDE

It had been the first place where slaves were auctioned and some of the exhibits include skeletons, artwork and craft items made by Africans who were brought here to be traded. Admission is € 1.50.

Church of St. Sebastian (Igreja de Sao Sebastiao)

Rua Conselheiro Joaquim Machado, Lagos 8600, Portugal

The church's most memorable feature must surely be the ossuary, which features various bones and skulls embedded into the walls. Although only three storeys high, the bell tower gives an elevated view of the historic town center, the beach and Bensafrim River. Admission is € 2.

Church of St. Anthony (Igreja de Santo Antonio)

Rua General Alberto da Silveira, Lagos 8600-594,

Portugal

Tel: 282 762 301

The detailed golden artwork featured within the church is one of its attractions, but these days it functions more as a museum than a place of worship.

The collection on display includes artwork, engravings and even ancient Roman artefacts. Some of its art treasures are specifically dedicated to St Anthony. Admission is € 3.

ALGARVE TRAVEL GUIDE

Zoo Lagos

Quinta Figueiras - Sítio do Medronhal

Barão de S. João

Lagos - Algarve – Portugal 8600

Tel: 282 680 100

http://www.zoolagos.com

Lagos Zoo strives to combine conservation with education and houses its animals within beautiful and environmentally suitable habitats. Some of the residents include gibbons, lemurs, marmosets, bobcats, prairie dogs, a pygmy hippo, meerkat, wallabi and various species of cranes, swans, hornbills and turkeys. There are also animals such as horses, ponies, donkeys, pot-bellied pigs, goats, guinea pigs, llamas and a petting zoo for kids. The focus is on smaller animals, but the grounds also includes a variety of flora from around the world. Admission is €14 for adults.

🌍 Tavira

The history of Tavira dates back about 4000 years, to 2000 BC and it is easy to see why. The Gilão River forms a pleasant backdrop to this town's scenery, but must have served as a trade artery in earlier times.

The market hall is now the setting of several shops and restaurants and a prominade with attractive pavillion and shaded benches for a moment's relaxation.

A low, arched structure known widely as the Roman bridge has on closer inspection been revealed to be of Moorish manufacture, dating back to the 12th century.

ALGARVE TRAVEL GUIDE

Nowadays it is a pedestrian only crossing. The surrounding architecture dates back to the 18th century, after the earthquake of 1755. The bridge also includes a monument for the fallen heroes of Portugal's struggle for independence between 1383 and 1385.

A few kilometers outside Tavira you will find Pego do Inferno. This relaxing spot in nature is basically a waterfall that empties into a pool at Santo Estêvã. Another attraction of Tavira is the Rio Formosa with one of its barrier islands being Tavira Island. Its wide beach area is regarded as one of the best beaches of the Algarve, and can be reached by ferry. The island also has camping facilities and restaurants.

ALGARVE TRAVEL GUIDE

Tavira Castle

The partial remains of the Moorish castle makes an imposing sight in Tavira's historical section. The first fortification to occupy the site may date back as far as 800 BC, to the time of the Phoenicians. Captured from the Moors in 1239, the castle was gifted to the Order of the Knights of Santiago in 1342, but returned to the King after three decades.

It was rebuilt towards the end of the thirteenth century as a strategy against increased pirate activity. Unfortunately, it suffered serious damage during the earthquake of 1755.

What remains of the fort are three walls, two square towers and one octagon-shaped tower. A small garden can be found within the courtyard. The site is allegedly haunted by the spirit of a young Moorish woman who had been the daughter of the last Muslim governor, Aben-Fabila. The castle's remaining features command a great view of Tavira. Admission is free.

🌎 Portimão

Portimão is located where the Arade River empties into the sea, making it the ideal location for a port, especially to a region as focused on maritime affairs as the Algarve. The marina has mooring space for well over 600 vessels. Here too, you will find shops, restaurants, bars and prime residential real estate. Two fortresses on opposite banks of the Arade, Santa Catarina and São João were constructed in the 1500s to protect port interests. Another guardian is the lighthouse on the Ferragudo Peninsula.

ALGARVE TRAVEL GUIDE

The city boasts one of the most popular beaches of the Algarve, Praia da Rocha. With excellent facilities, it can get quite crowded at the height of summer. It carries Blue Flag status, as does several other beaches in the area, such as Praia do Vau, Praia do AlvorPoente and Praia dos TrêsIrmãos, which is rendered distinct by a striking rock formation nearby.

To catch a glimpse of the old ways, visit the traditional fishing village of Ferragudo, which is just opposite the river from Portimão. A charming place to pause is in the old district of Portimão is the fountain near the old market hall. The area is a stop on the Lisbon to Dakar Rally. In summer, Portimão hosts a beach soccer challenge.

ALGARVE TRAVEL GUIDE

 Faro

Although few buildings in Faro survived the earthquake of 1755 intact, the city does feature ruins of both Arab and Roman descent. The older part of town still has remnants of the Roman walls and the open square preserves the layout of a Roman forum.

In the oldest district, you could explore Faro's marina or Jardim Manuel Bivar, a botanical garden where visitors and locals enjoy strolling. Here too, you will find a popular pedestrian shopping region. The district features various townhouses in the Jugendstil architectural style.

Considering the region's illustrious maritime heritage, the Naval Museum is certainly worth a visit. The church of NossoSenhora is famous for its style of gold-leaf covered

ALGARVE TRAVEL GUIDE

woodwork and also the Chapel of Bones, which holds the earthly remains of around 1200 monks.

Faro serves as administrative capital and is located near the region's main airport. It has also been the seat of the Bishop of the Algarve since the latter part of the 1500s, only a few decades after it officially became a city in 1540. As many religious buildings in the Algarve, the Sé Cathedral still preserves elements of the mosque that once occupied its place.

The beachfront area of Faro forms part of the Ria Formosa. The main beach area, Praia do Faro-Mar, is accessible via a bridge. Another beach, Praia da Barreta, can only be reached by ferry.

Faro Archaeological Museum

Tel: 289 803 604

The Faro Archaeological Museum is located within a convent constructed in the early 1500s. The architecture is in itself something to admire. Collected within you will discover various finds from the area, including Roman mosaics, sculptures and relics of religious significance. The paintings exhibited date mainly from the 16th and 17th century and include works of Portuguese and Italian origin. There are also objects from the Moorish period.

ALGARVE TRAVEL GUIDE

Igreja do Carmo Church / Capela dos Ossos (Chapel of Bones)

Within the chapel of bones you will find row upon row of skulls. This ornate but grisly decoration is provided by the remains of monks who had been buried in the cemetery that once occupied this site. It was built in 1816.

Estoi Palace

Rua de Sao Jose, 8005 Estoi

Tel: 289 990 150

Commissioned by José Francisco da Silva, the Viscount of Estoi in the late 1800s, the lavish palace was eventually completed in 1909. It features the Rococo style, but also includes beautiful tileworkThe site is currently being transformed into a hotel.

Milreu

Off the N2, about 20 minutes out of Faro, Estoi

The ruins at Milreu date back to Roman times. The complex includes a temple, winepress and baths as well as an extensive plumbing system.

Water is a recurrent theme in the decorative art, of which the preserved fish mosaics are a good example. In the 3rd century its function shifted from villa to farm. Towards the 6th century, it became a church and after the 10th century it served as Muslim cemetery.

ALGARVE TRAVEL GUIDE

A visitor's center near the actual digs displays how the Romans lived.

Admission to the site is €2.

🌍 Ria Formosa

The Ria Formosa is an extended lagoon created by a system of barrier islands and peninsulas stretching from Manta Rota to Garrão, a distance of about 60 km.

Punctuated by a series of sand dunes, sand bars and isles, this area was formed with the oceanic upheavals of the earthquake of 1755. There are five main islands, namely Faro, Barreta, Culatra, Armona and Tavira.

ALGARVE TRAVEL GUIDE

The area is utilized in various ways by the Algarve people. Salt deposits are harvested near Tavira, as the region is relatively uncontaminated by pollutants. Other products of the area are fish and shellfish. The region accounts for 80 percent of Portugal's exports in clams.

The maze-like formations have six points of entry towards the beach region of which five are natural. These features offer protection to a variety of species, making it an ideal breeding ground. Endangered species, such as sea horses and chameleons also find sanctuary here.

Due to the large number of migratory and nesting water birds such as flamingo and heron found here, it is popular with bird watching enthusiasts. Another native of this territory is the Portuguese water dog. These friendly animals often served as invaluable aids to fishermen, but faced extinction in recent years. Fortunately their numbers have recovered somewhat.

The Ria Formosa has been a National Park since 1987. The region combines duneland, marshland and woodland and includes a number of interesting hiking trails. Faro Island is accessible by road and there is a regular bus service to the island. Armona Island and Tavira Island boasts some excellent beaches and can be reached by ferry or water taxi.

🌐 Vilamoura

The resort of Vilamoura encompasses a casino and marina, a series of superior beaches, and a great selection of shops, restaurants and nightspots. The nearby vicinity offers a variety of outdoor activities which include horse-riding, tennis, water sports and golf.

The facilities on offer for the golfing enthusiasts are of a particularly high standard. Vilamoura lies just off the Golden Triangle, a region well known for its luxury housing and outstanding golf courses. The Portuguese Masters Golf Tournament is held in Vilamoura.

From the marina, you can organize leisurely coastal cruises or big game fishing excursions. There are plenty of opportunities for hiking or cycling in the area as well.

🌐 Albufeira

Within a few decades, Albufeira grew from humble fishing village to populous resort town. Its premier beach, Praia

ALGARVE TRAVEL GUIDE

dos Pescadores is located near the historical part of town and still has a section set aside for fishing boats. The other beach, Praia do Túnel is named after its access point - a tunnel through which all beachgoers must pass.

From the modern sculptures incorporated in several of the town's traffic circles to the picturesque square of the old district, Albufeira is easy on the eye.

Two main commercial arteries of the town are Rua 5 de Outubro and Ave Dr. Francisco SáCarneiro, also known as The Strip, which is favored by English-speaking visitors and residents. As Albufeira is a popular tourist destination, English is often heard, seen and used.

ALGARVE TRAVEL GUIDE

A colorful feature of Albufeira is its marina. The surrounding buildings are painted in a combination of orange, pink, green amd blue. It was created through the demolition of a natural rock wall. An important landmark of Albufeira, its clocktower, once served a very different function. It had been part of a castle.

🌐 Monchique

Unlike the coastal regions, Monchique is still relatively undiscovered by tourist trends. It is located between two hills, the Picota and the Fóia and provides a pleasant mix of narrow, cobbled lanes full of character and beautiful scenery.

Nearby is Fóia, at 902m, the highest point of the Serra de Monchique hills. It is the site of a radar station. The view

ALGARVE TRAVEL GUIDE

here is very wide, including sights such as Cape St. Vincent, the southern most point of Europe, the city Faro and Serra da Arrabida.

Surrounding features of the area include an aqueduct, waterfalls and impressive granite structures.

The most striking element of the Monchique central square is an old Moorish water wheel. Fans of ceramic art may wish to visit Casa da Nogueira, the birthplace of LeonelTeo, a Portuguese exponent of this art form. The Quinta de São Bento, formerly a summer retreat for the royal family, now serves as hotel and restaurant.

There is also a sulphuric hot spring, Fonte Santa with the adjacent spa at Caldas de Monchique. This has been

ALGARVE TRAVEL GUIDE

known since the Roman era. A Franciscan monastery from the 1600s nestles near the town. The area is famous for Medronho, a local spirit distilled from arbutus berries.

🌎 Silves

Silves was probably founded around 1000 BC and was utililized by both the Romans and the Visigoths during their reign of the region. Via the Arade River, and its proximity to Portimão, Silves grew to an important trading town. The Moors raised Silves to the status of capital, but were unable to hold it for longer than a few centuries.

Several towns and cities in the Algarve possess a crossing known as Ponte Romana or the Old Roman Bridge and Silves is no different. The design, composed of several low arches, is fairly typical, but it is more likely that it was constructed in the Middle Ages, despite the name. Today it serves pedestrian traffic only. A small market trades nearby.

Various buildings in Silves can be admired for the tiled facades often associated with Portuguese architecture. Silves Cathedral, with its gothic doors dates back to the 13th century, when the reconquesta of Portugal brought new religious fervor to the Algarve. A later church, the Igreja da Misericórdia, displays a later variation on the gothic theme. This church also has an art gallery.

Silves Castle

R. do Castelo, Silves, Algarve, Portugal

Silves Castle occupies a prime strategic position near the

ALGARVE TRAVEL GUIDE

mouth of the Arade River.

This site may have served as fortification as far back as the time of the Romans, but the present castle is believed to date back to the period just prior to the Moorish conquest, most likely around 715. It has a lively history. After the Moorish conquest, it was briefly taken by Fernando I, King of Leon in 1060, before falling a second time to the Moors.

In 1189, a Portuguese Christian army, aided by Crusaders from England, Germany and Flanders regained Silves Castle for King Sancho I of Portugal. Later Moorish attempts to occupy the castle proved unsuccessful. Sancho disarmed the structure, but it was rebuilt and refurnished during the mid to late 1300s. The

ALGARVE TRAVEL GUIDE

earthquake of 1755 wrought significant damage to the castle, but it was still declared a national monument in 1910, being the largest castle of its kind in the Algarve.

The layout includes a citadel, battlement walls and a total of eleven square towers. It is made of a combination of red sandstone and taipa, a mixture often used in Moorish structures. There is a sad legend associated with the El MouraEncantada, where a Moorish princess allegedly still mourns her lost sweetheart.

From its elevated location, the castle ramparts command a spectacular view of the rest of Silves. Admission is € 2.50.

ALGARVE TRAVEL GUIDE

Cork Museum

Fábrica do Inglés, Rua Gregório Mascarenhas

Phone: 242 440 480

Silves falls within the region where cork is cultivated and processed and an interesting stop to make is the cork museum. This was an important industry of Silves up to the beginning of the 20th century and once employed thousands of townsfolk in multiple factories.

Archaeological Museum

14 Rua das Portas de Loulé, 8300-139 Silves

Tel: 282 444 832

Since the earliest human activity within this region dates back to prehistoric times, there are many interesting

ALGARVE TRAVEL GUIDE

Palaeolithic and Neolithic finds on display here, alongside artefacts from Roman, Moorish and more recent history. The remaining wall of a well from the Middle Ages forms part of the building. Admission is € 2.

🌍 Loule

Loule occupies an expanse of land that begins at the Algarve coast and stretches up to 12 km inland. It combines healthy commercial growth with the old world beauty of its historic district where reminders of Moorish architecture can still be seen.

One of the city's big attractions is its annual festival. In February, crowds line the street to watch a parade of colorful floats and super sized mannikins. The event attracts many visitors.

ALGARVE TRAVEL GUIDE

A harmonious, but modern water feature decorates the Largo de Gago Coutinho or central square of Loule. In this area you will also find the market hall, an elegant building of Moorish origin. This is the scene of a weekly Saturday market where lace, copperware, leather ware and earthenware can be purchased. By comparison, the town hall is a building of simple geometric features.

One of the town's better known residents was the Portuguese poet, António Aleixo. Although unassuming, his thoughts and writings left an intellectual legacy that is not only recognized in his own country, but also in other Portuguese speaking nations, such as Brazil. He spent his last years in Loule and today bronze statue of Aleixo

ALGARVE TRAVEL GUIDE

sits at a table opposite the Calcinha café, as he often did in life.

Three towers and some walls are what remains of the town's Moorish castle, which dates back to the 13th century. It now functions as a museum and houses the town archives.

Some of the key buildings of Loule attest to a policy of reclaiming and recycling its history. The arched Portas do Céu or town gate was once part of the castle complex. Igreja Matriz de São Clemente or the town church was built in the 13th century, incorporating the portal of a mosque that had once occupied the site and it includes a separate belfry of granite that was originally a Moorish minaret.

ALGARVE TRAVEL GUIDE

Convento do Espírito Santo

Rua Vice- Almirante Cândido dos Reis, Loulé

Tel: 289 400 600

Although built in the 17th century, the Monastery of the Holy Spirit suffered significant damage during the devastating earthquake that hit Portugal in 1755. The epicenter struck Lisbon, but its impact was also felt in the Algarve and beyond. The building was reconstructed in the 18th century. It now hosts an art collection.

Neolithic Sites

The Iberian Peninsula is rich with the remains of Neolithic culture and the Algarve boasts several locations with interesting finds. At Alacar, various ancient funeral sites have been uncovered. The most striking of these, known

ALGARVE TRAVEL GUIDE

as Monument 7, is a well-preserved cairn of stones arranged in a circular tholos shape.

Montes dos Amantes has a different type of heritage from the past. The site is a garden of menhirs, dating back to between 3,000 and 4,000 BC. It is believed that they originated from another location, but were transported here. The sizes vary and some include decorative details. There are also footprints of early humans preserved in stone. The site is located between Vila do Bispo and Sagres.

There is a particularly extensive collection of menhirs near Praia da Ingrina. They are believed to be associated with the fertility cults of the prehistoric inhabitants.

ALGARVE TRAVEL GUIDE

Budget Tips

 Accommodation

While the accommodation tariffs in the Algarve is generally very affordable, it should be born in mind that many hotels add a special levy for a stay of less than three nights.

ALGARVE TRAVEL GUIDE

Tivoli Lagos Hotel

Rua Antonio Crisogono Santos, Lagos 8600-678,

Portugal

http://www.algarvetivolilagos.com/

The Tivoli Hotel in Lagos offers you the opportunity to enjoy a variety of conveniences at affordable prices. There are three restaurants, with different specialities as well as a Pool Bar to provide refreshments. Other on-site entertainment includes a games room with facilities for table tennis, darts, cards, snooker and chess, a sauna, a Jacuzzi, three outdoor swimming pools, plus a heated indoor one and also a fitness center.

Some of the nearby attractions for visitors include Lagos Zoo, Aqualand and the Slide & Splash water park. Meia

ALGARVE TRAVEL GUIDE

Praia beach is right by the hotel. Facilities are wheelchair friendly. Rooms include a safe, a mini-bar, air-conditioning, satellite TV and Wifi Internet. Breakfast is included in the price. Accommodation begins at €58 a night.

Casa das Oliveiras

Montes da Vala,

Silves 8300-044, Portugal

Tel: 282 342 115

http://www.casa-das-oliveiras.com/

Casa das Oliveiras is a small, but highly rated guesthouse in Silves. The garden provides a tranquil spot to relax amid olive trees and cork oaks. There is also a pool and a terrace where breakfast is served. A well-equipped

ALGARVE TRAVEL GUIDE

kitchenette is available for use by the guests. Casa das Oliveiras offers facilities for table tennis, satellite TV and free Wifi. All rooms include a bathroom. Accommodation varies between € 27 and € 65.

Hotel Porta Nova

Rua Antonio Pinheiro,

Tavira 8800-323, Portugal

Tel: 282 423 770

Hotel Porta Nova is conveniently located near the historical district, public transport and plenty of bars and restaurants. All rooms feature en-suite bathroom facilities and include a mini-bar, safe and satellite TV. There are swimming pools, a game room and a well-equipped sauna that offers steam, Jacuzzi and massage services.

The reception area has free Wifi Internet. The hotel reception is also a great source of tourist information. Accommodation begins at €20 a night.

Hotel Sol Algarve

Rua Infante D. Henrique, 52,

Faro 8000-363, Portugal

Tel: 289 895 700

http://www.hotelsolalgarve.com/

When Hotel Sol Algarve was enlarged in 2004, its grounds were found to contain the remains of Roman ruins. The hotel is located near the train station and the historical district and boasts a friendly, attractive interior.

ALGARVE TRAVEL GUIDE

All rooms include en-suite bathrooms, air conditioning, cable TV and free Internet. Breakfast is included in the price. Accommodation varies from €35 to €80 per night.

Hotel Ibis Faro

E.N. 125 Pontes de Marchil,

Faro 8000-770, Portugal

Tel: 289 893 800

http://www.ibis.com/gb/hotel-1593-ibis-faro/

The Hotel Ibis Faro boasts a bright and modern decor. It is located near the beach, as well as the enigmatic Ria Formosa Nature Reserve, which is one of the great natural attractions of the Algarve. The hotel has a lovely swimming pool and all rooms have air conditioning,

ALGARVE TRAVEL GUIDE

television, free Wifi Internet and bathroom facilities.

The price includes a large and extensive breakfast buffet selection. The hotel is a participant in the Le Club Accorhotels loyalty program. Accommodation begins at €35.

🌎 Places to Eat

Oasis

Marina de Lagos,

Lagos, Portugal

Located on the Lagos Marina, Oasis is English owned and serves a combination of Portuguese and International cuisine. The cafe is open for breakfast, lunch and supper. Try the full English Breakfast or pick from the choice of

ALGARVE TRAVEL GUIDE

toasted sandwiches and baguettes, gammon steaks, burgers, pasta and fish and chips. On Friday nights, try the special deal, which allows you to enjoy a meal and drink for only €7.95.

Marco's Bistro

Dunas de Alvor, Loja 16, Alvor,

Portimao, Portugal

Tel: 282 457 548

http://www.marcosalvor.com/

Marco's Bistro provides a friendly setting for enjoying good food at affordable prices. There are various special deals such as the Poolside Special, which comprises the choice of a burger or hot dog plus beverage for €3.50 or the Sunday lunch for €10.95. Some of the dinner

ALGARVE TRAVEL GUIDE

highlights include Spicy Chilli Con Carne, homemade lasagne and the Horseshoe Gammon Steak. Lunchtime menu items include sandwiches ranged from €2.00 to €3.95, salads, hot dogs, burgers, French fries and baked potato. There is a breakfast menu as well. Marco's also offers free Wifi access.

Fat Cats Diner

Rodrimar Apartments

Rua Dumfermline,

Albufeira 8200, Portugal

Tel: 966 799 779

The Fat Cats Diner presents a well maintained exterior and boosts atmosphere with regular events such as quizzes and karaoke. The food is well-prepared and great value for money. The menu includes salads, sandwiches, baked potato, with a variety of fillings, fish and chips, gammon steak and English breakfast. Menu items range from €4 for a breakfast to around €10 for the fish and chips.

Restaurante a Taska

Rua do Alportel 38,

Faro

Tel: 289 824 739

For an eatery that is a little off the tourist track, try a local favorite in Faro, namely Restaurante a Taska. On the menu you will find regional specialties such as eel stew and pork with clams. Expect to pay between €13 and €16 for meals and drinks.

ALGARVE TRAVEL GUIDE

Restaurante da Bairrada

Vale Caranguejo,

Tavira 8800-453, Portugal

Tel: 281 324 467

Restaurante da Bairrada is popular with locals and the expat community of Tavira. Some of the menu highlights include suckling pig, monkfish kebabs and the popular steak on a stone, although the restaurant also serves lighter meals such as omelettes, salads and sandwiches. Expect to pay between €15 and €20 per person.

🌐 Shopping

Shopping in Albufeira

There are two main areas you should visit when planning a shopping excursion in Albufeira. Rua 5 de Outubro is located near the tunnel that leads to the beach and here you can expect an interesting mix of clothing shops and craft traders. In the holiday months, there will also be a number of temporary stalls. A great place for local crafts is Infante Dom Henrique House at RuaCândido do Reis 30, which sells hand-woven baskets, ceramics and painted tiles.

The centrally located Belle Vista Shopping Center is anchored by two supermarkets, but also features a variety of smaller shops and food outlets. The Av. Dr. Francisco SáCarneiro is known as The Strip and the business in this area focuses more on tourist trade. There are several restaurants, bars as well as souvenir shops where you can buy the usual T-shirts and other keepsakes.

ALGARVE TRAVEL GUIDE

A fashion outlet nearby that may be worth exploring is Oceana Boutique on Galarias Nova Oura. Catering in ladies fashion, you would stand a good chance of discovering something here that is both attractive and a little different, sometimes at very reasonable prices. The Algarve Shopping Mall, which is just outside the town, has a selection of over 80 different shops. Over 25 of these cater in fashion and clothing. The mall is off the EN125 highway.

Shopping in Lagos

A street highly recommended for browsing and shopping in Lagos is Rua 25 de Abril, where there is a particularly good selection of outlets offering pottery, ceramics and "azulejos", the distinctive blue tiles used in the mosaics that decorate many a building in the Algarve. Another location, just outside Lagos is Hipercerâmica Paraíso Lda, which sells pottery, leatherwork, cork products and tiles. It can be found on the way to Sagres at EN125, Raposeira which is west of Lagos. Near the marina, you could visit the Lagos Marina Gift Shop, for clothing and keepsakes of this area.

Shopping in Faro

The Forum Algarve on Av. Cáceres Monteiro (http://www.forumalgarve.net/) is a large shopping center near the city Faro, which boasts a beautiful exterior with tiling detail. The complex includes various fashion and home decor shops as well as a supermarket, cinemas and a large food court on the second floor.

ALGARVE TRAVEL GUIDE

One street in Faro with plenty of shopping opportunity is the Rua do Santo Antonio. Do check out Carminho at number 29 and Casa Branca at number 10 for locally crafted items. Other streets worth browsing through are Rua de Francisco Gomes and Rua de Portugal. There is also a market, the Mercado de Faro, that trades every day in the city centre.

Casa das Portas in Tavira

Rua Dr Augusto Silva Carvalho,

Tavira, Portugal

http://www.casadasportas.com/

Located near the Roman bridge, Casa das Portas showcases a beautiful range of original, locally crafted items. Items range from jewellery to ornaments, handbags, ceramics and art prints. The 'Portas' series by Jane Gibbin, which features photographs of doors and windows around Tavira is a prominent theme of the shop.

Gypsy Markets

Nearly every town or city has at least one weekly or monthly market, selling fresh produce, crafts or sometimes antiques. The one in Loulé sells various crafted items such as baskets and ceramics. It trades every second Saturday of the month at Cortelha. Lagos hosts a market on the first Saturday at the municiple stadium, but there is also a fleamarket on the second Saturday at Chinicato.

Tavira's gypsy market is on the third Saturday in Rua Vale Carangueijo. Portimao has a market on the first Monday

ALGARVE TRAVEL GUIDE

at Parque de Feiras e Exposições, while Silves has a market near the cemetery on the third Monday of each month.

Know Before You Go

Entry Requirements

By virtue of the Schengen agreement, travellers from other countries in the European Union do not need a visa when visiting Portugal. Travellers from the UK, Bulgaria, Croatia, Cyprus, Romania and Ireland are also exempted from needing a visa and visitors from Australia, Canada and the USA, do not require a visa, provided that their stay does not exceed 90 days. Travellers requiring a Schengen visa will be able to enter Portugal with it multiple times within a 6 month period, if their stay does not exceed 90 days. They may need to prove that they have sufficient funds available to cover the duration of their stay in Portugal. For a stay exceeding 90 days, non-EU visitors will need to apply for a temporary residence permit.

Health Insurance

Citizens of other EU countries as well as residents from Switzerland, Norway, Iceland and Liechtenstein and the UK are covered for health care in Portugal with the European Health Insurance Card (EHIC), which can be applied for free of charge. If you need a Schengen visa for your stay in Portugal, you will also be required to obtain proof of health insurance for the duration of your stay (that offers at least €37,500 coverage), as part of their visa application. Visitors from Canada or the USA should check whether their regular health insurance covers travel and arrange for extended health insurance if required.

🌍 Travelling with Pets

When travelling with pets from another country in the European Union, certain requirements have to be met. The animal will need to be microchipped and up to date on their rabies shots. Additionally you should have applied for a EU pet passport from your country of origin. If you are planning to visit Portugal from outside the European Union, a health certificate in English or Portuguese needs to be submitted by a certified vet. For the non-commercial transport of animals to Portugal from non-European Union countries, the relevant authority at the Portuguese point of entry needs to be informed in writing at least 48 hours in advance of the arrival of the animal.

🌍 Airports

Apart from the airports in Lisbon, Faro and Oporto, Portugal's busiest routes are to the islands of the Azores and the Canaries. **Lisbon Portela Airport** (LIS) is the busiest international airport in Portugal and connects travellers with its capital,

Lisbon. **Francisco de Sá Carneiro Airport** (OPO) near Oporto is Portugal's second busiest airport. It is a focus city for EasyJet and Ryanair. **Faro Airport** (FAO) is particularly busy during the summer months, when it provides access to the Algarve region. **Madeira Airport** (FNC), with its notoriously short runway, was once considered one of the most dangerous airports. Located in Santa Cruz near Funchal, it provides access to the island of Madeira from destinations in France, Germany, Finland, the Netherlands and the UK. Another important airport in the Azores is **Horta International Airport** (HOR), which provides a vital link to the archipelago's outlying islands, such as Flores and Corvo. **Santa Maria Airport** (SMA) on the island of Santa Maria in the Azores once served as an important hub for the facilitation of trans-Atlantic connections, particularly in the post-World War Two era. Although it has in recent years slipped into a more regional role, it still has amenities suitable for transatlantic aircraft.

Airlines

TAP Portugal is the flag-carrying airline of Portugal. Founded in 1946, it flies travellers to 88 different destinations in 38 countries including Amsterdam, Barcelona, Madrid, Berlin, Frankfurt, Munich, Oslo, Marrakech, Miami, Luanda, Maputo, Moscow, Casablanca, Panama and Rio de Janeiro. SATA Air

ALGARVE TRAVEL GUIDE

Açores is a small airline based in the Azores, which operates scheduled flights as a carrier of passengers, cargo and mail. In the late 1990s, it acquired OceanAir and renamed it SATA International. Sata provides scheduled flights connecting Ponta Delgada to Lisbon, Madeira Island and Porto and also operates trans-Atlantic routes to Faro and Toronto. Portugalia began operations as a regional airline in the 1980s, flying domestic routes within Portugal as well as to Italy, France, Spain, Germany and Morocco. It was acquired by TAP Portugal in 2006.

Lisbon Portela Airport serves as a hub for Portugalia and TAP Portugal, as well as White Airlines, which operates mainly chartered flights on behalf of Portuguese tour operators. It is also a focus city for EasyJet and Ryanair. SATA Air Açores and SATA International are based at João Paulo II Airport in the Azores.

Currency

The currency of Portugal is the Euro. It is issued in notes in denominations of €500, €200, €100, €50, €20, €10 and €5. Coins are issued in denominations of €2, €1, 50c, 20c, 10c, 5c, 2c and 1c.

ALGARVE TRAVEL GUIDE

🌐 Banking & ATMs

Using ATMs in Portugal to withdraw money is simple if your ATM card is compatible with the MasterCard/Cirrus or Visa/Plus networks. Portuguese ATM machines are also known as Multibanco and will be identified with the logo, MB. There is a good distribution of machines available throughout Portugal. In general ATMs will give you the most beneficial rate of exchange, although some bank groups may levy an additional fee on international transactions. European ATMs are configured for 4-digit PIN numbers.

🌐 Credit Cards

Visa and MasterCard are widely accepted in many Portuguese businesses. Some businesses also accept American Express and will indicate this by displaying its logo. Other credit cards valid in Portugal include Diners Club, Maestro, Europay and JCB. Credit cards issued in Europe are smart cards that that are fitted with a microchip and require a PIN for each transaction. If you still have an older magnetic strip card, you may find that some facilities are not configured to process your transaction. Do remember to advise your bank or credit card company of your travel plans before leaving home.

🌐 Tourist Taxes

The city of Lisbon introduced a tourist tax in 2015 which will charge visitors €1 per night for the first 7 days of their stay in Lisbon. The tax does not apply to minor children. A review of this policy is due in 2019.

🌐 Reclaiming VAT

If you are not from the European Union, you can claim back VAT (Value Added Tax) paid on your purchases in Portugal. The VAT rate in Portugal is 23 percent and this can be claimed back on your purchases, if certain conditions are met. Only purchases of €60 and over qualify for a VAT refund. You will be asked for proof (usually in the form of a passport) that your normal residence is outside the European Union. Participating shops will clearly display that they offer a VAT-free service. A form needs to be filled in by the shop assistant. At customs of your last port within the European Union (which need not be the place where you bought the goods), you should submit this form. The goods and sales invoice will be inspected before the form is stamped and approved.

ALGARVE TRAVEL GUIDE

🌐 Tipping Policy

A service fee is usually included in restaurant bills in Portugal, but it is accepted to leave an additional 5-10 percent gratuity. It is also customary to tip taxi drivers 5 to 10 percent of the fee.

🌐 Mobile Phones

Most EU countries, including Portugal uses the GSM mobile service. This means that most UK phones and some US and Canadian phones and mobile devices will work in Portugal. However, phones using the CDMA network will not be compatible. While you could check with your service provider about coverage before you leave, using your own service in roaming mode will involve additional costs. The alternative is to purchase a Portuguese SIM card to use during your stay in Portugal. Portugal has three mobile networks. They are MEO (formerly known as TMN), Vodafone and NOS (formerly known as Optimus). MEO is the largest service provider that offers the best coverage and SIM cards are available from €2.50. Data only rates begin at €10 for 10GB, valid for 3 days. Vodafone has a vendor at Porto airport and you can get a data only SIM card for €2.50 or voice and data. The data rate begins at €1.99 for 100 Mb. Bear in mind that for the data only package there are two different rates, a 7 day rate and a 30 day rate, which cannot be interchanged. NOS is the smallest of the Portuguese networks. They offer a SIM card for €2.50, with various top-up packages ranging from €1.99 for 30 MB that expires within 24 hours to €7.99 for 1 GB that is valid for one month.

🌍 Dialling Code

The international dialling code for Portugal is +351.

🌍 Emergency Numbers

Police: 112

Medical Emergencies: 112

Fire Rescue: 112

Forest Fires: 117

24 Hour Health line for emergencies: 808 242 424

Sea Rescue: 214 401 919

Maritime Police: 210 911 100

MasterCard: 800 811 272

Visa: 800 811 107

ALGARVE TRAVEL GUIDE

🌐 Public Holidays

1 January: New Year's Day

March/April: Good Friday

25 April: Freedom Day

1 May: Worker's Day

10 June: Portugal Day

15 August: Feast of the Assumption

8 December: Immaculate Conception

25 December: Christmas Day

🌐 Time Zone

In the winter season from the end of October to the end of March, Portugal's official time is the same as Greenwich Mean Time/Coordinated Universal Time (GMT/UTC); Eastern Standard Time (North America) -4; Pacific Standard Time (North America) -7.

🌐 Daylight Savings Time

Clocks are set forward one hour on the last Sunday of March and set back one hour on the last Sunday of October for Daylight Savings Time.

ALGARVE TRAVEL GUIDE

🌐 School Holidays

The academic year in Portugal begins in mid September and ends in mid June, but there may be different schedules for private and international schools. The summer holiday is from mid June to mid September, although the exact times may vary according to region. There are short breaks between Christmas and New Year and also during Easter and for the Carnival season in February or March.

🌐 Trading Hours

Most shops in Portugal trade from 9am to 7pm on weekdays and until 1pm on Saturdays, but at some shopping centers, trading hours may be extended to midnight. Shops may also stay open on Saturday afternoons and even Sundays during the Christmas season. Certain shops close for lunch between 1 and 3pm. Banks are open from 8.30am to 3pm on weekdays and the post office is open from 9am to 6pm, Monday to Friday, with extended weekend hours available in at some branches, for example at the airport. Pharmacies trade from 9am to 7pm, but details about the nearest all night pharmacy will usually also be signposted.

🌐 Driving Laws

The Portuguese drive on the right hand side of the road. A driver's licence from any of the European Union member countries is valid in Portugal. If visiting from a non-EU country, you will need to obtain an International Driving Permit to be able to drive in Portugal. The minimum driving age in Portugal is 18. The speed limit in Portugal is 120km per hour for freeways, 90km per hour for rural roads and 50km per hour in urban areas. The alcohol limit in Portugal is below 0.5 g/l. Toll roads in Portugal can be paid at dispensing booths or alternately, you could obtain a permanent or temporary electronic device that will be identified as a toll pass. This can be paid via credit card or ATM. Children under the age of 12 are not allowed to ride in the front seat. It is also illegal to drive with head phones or when using a mobile phone. Make sure that the vehicle you are using is up to date on road tax, fully covered by third party insurance and carries standard emergency gear such as warning triangles and a reflective safety vest. If older than four years, the car needs to have a valid IPO (Inspecção Periódica Obrigatória) as proof of roadworthiness.

🌐 Drinking Laws

In Portugal, the legal purchase age is 16 for beer and wine and 18 for spirits. The sale of alcohol in bars and restaurants is forbidden after midnight and public drinking after 2am.

🌐 Smoking Laws

In 2008, smoking was banned in all public places in Portugal, including work spaces, public transport, schools, libraries, museums, indoor car parks, indoor sports facilities, bars, cafes and discos. Restaurants with a floor space exceeding 100 sq. m. can allocate an enclosed area of not more than 30 percent with adequate ventilation as a smoker's area. The minimum age for smoking is 18. Persons who violate anti-smoking laws can be liable for a fine of between €50 and €750.

🌐 Electricity

Electricity: 230 volts
Frequency: 50 Hz
Portuguese electricity sockets are compatible with the Type C Euro adaptor and Type F plugs, which features two round pins or prongs. If travelling from the USA, you will need a power converter or transformer to convert the voltage from 230 to 110,

to avoid damage to your appliances. The latest models of many laptops, camcorders, mobile phones and digital cameras are dual-voltage with a built in converter.

🌐 Tourist Information (TI)

There are several tourist information outlets in Lisbon, the capital. The Lisbon Welcome Center is at 15 Rua do Arsenal, but there is also a tourist information outlet at Lisbon Portela Airport and Palacio Foz, in Praca dos Restauradores. The Cascais tourist information office is at Rua Visconde da Luz and there is also a tourist information outlet at Avenue Miguel Bombarda in Sintra. The Porto Convention Bureau at Ponte Luís I promotes tourism in Porto.

🌐 Food & Drink

Fish and seafood are important ingredients of Portuguese cuisine. One of the most popular dishes is bacalhau or salted cod, which can be found in a huge selection of regional varieties. Sardines - grilled or fried, is another national favorite and makes common street food in Lisbon, particularly in June when the Santa Antonio festival takes place. The traditional Portuguese soup is Caldo Verde, with a base of onion and potato and another signature dish is feijoada, a rich and meaty

ALGARVE TRAVEL GUIDE

bean stew. Chouriço is a Portuguese pork sausage similar to the Spanish chorizo and it has a kosher counterpart in alheira de mirandela. Originally devised by Iberian Jews to fool the Inquisitors, the sausage may include veal, rabbit, chicken and duck.

Try Caldeirada de Enguias or eel stew from Aveiro or the seafood stew cataplana from the Algarve. In Porto, try the francesinha, a sandwich stuffed with ham, sausage and steak, smothered in cheese and then served with a signature tomato based sauce. The island of Madeira has plenty to offer, gastronomically speaking, ranging from meaty Espetada to Bolo de Mel or honey cake. The Azores boasts a selection of dairy products, including the well-known Queijo da Ilha which originates from the island, São Jorge. Here, too, seafood is popular, particularly octopus, mackerel and lamprey. Enjoy home-grown pineapples and the one-pot speciality cozida on São Miguel, while a slow-cooked Alcatra pot-roast may tantalize your taste buds on Terçeira. Azorean sweets include Massa Sovada or Portuguese sweet bread, and Malasadas.

Port wine, also known as Vinho de Porto, is a sweet, fortified wine made of red grapes grown exclusively in the Douro Valley of northern Portugal. It is traditionally enjoyed after dinner and served with cheese. Madeira is famous for wines such as Bual, Sercial, Malmsey and Verdelho. You should also try Poncho, a drink made from sugarcane rum, lemon juice and honey or ginja, a local liqueur distilled from cherries. Nikita, a blend of pineapple and vanilla can be enjoyed with or without alcohol. Try the distinctive wines from São Miguel and Pico in the Azores.

 Websites

https://www.visitportugal.com/en

http://portugal.com/

http://wikitravel.org/en/Portugal

http://www.insideportugaltravel.com/

http://www.portugal-live.com/

http://www.portugal-live.net/

http://www.travel-in-portugal.com/

Printed in Great Britain
by Amazon